D0516410

KENTUCKY

Past and Present

Colleen Ryckert Cook

rosen publishing's
rosen
central

New York

To all Kentucky students—past, present, and future

Published in 2011 by The Rosen Publishing Group, Inc.
29 East 21st Street, New York, NY 10010

Library of Congress Cataloging-in-Publication Data

Cook, Colleen Ryckert.
Kentucky: past and present / Colleen Ryckert Cook. — 1st ed.
    p. cm. — (The United States: past and present)
Includes bibliographical references and index.
ISBN 978-1-4358-9482-2 (library binding)
ISBN 978-1-4358-9509-6 (pbk.)
ISBN 978-1-4358-9543-0 (6-pack)
1. Kentucky—Juvenile literature. I. Title.
F451.3.C66 2010
976.9—dc22

20100025071

Manufactured in Malaysia

CPSIA Compliance Information: Batch #S10YA: For further information, contact Rosen Publishing, New York, New York, at 1-800-237-9932.

On the cover: Top left: The first commercial coal mine in Kentucky opened in 1820. Miners faced danger on the job every day. Top right: Kentucky is known for its horse ranches and green fields. Bottom: Mine That Bird takes the lead during the 2009 Kentucky Derby.

Contents

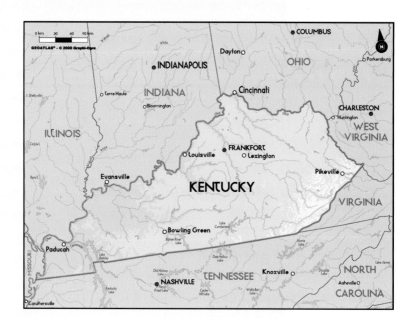

The Commonwealth of Kentucky is also called the Bluegrass State. In 1792, it became the fifteenth state to join the new United States of America. Its motto is "United We Stand, Divided We Fall."

Introduction

In the 1700s, adventurers explored America's unsettled land. They found wonders west of the Appalachian Mountains. Lush forests loomed over green meadows. Rainbows of wildflowers dotted the grasses. Animals grazed under blue skies. Rivers rushed through the land. The horizon stretched before them, rich and wild.

Daniel Boone declared it "a second paradise." Native people who hunted there had already given it other names. The Wyandot called it *kah-ten-tah-teh*, which means "land of tomorrow." Iroquois had a similar name, *kenhta-ke*, which means "meadow." The settlers who braved river currents and steep mountain trails called it their new home.

Today, lots of people live in Kentucky. They are musicians and miners. They are horse trainers and tobacco farmers. They are car builders and road workers. Kentucky has big cities and small towns. Modern adventurers hike cool mountain trails or ride horseback through sunny meadows. They explore plunging canyons, massive caves, and even wetlands.

Kentucky counts seven states as neighbors. In the north, Illinois, Indiana, and Ohio lie along the Ohio River. To the east are West Virginia and Virginia. Tennessee is south. Missouri lies west, across the Mississippi River.

It's easy to remember Kentucky's shape on the map. It looks like a person lying on the flat ground, using the Appalachians for a pillow and watching the clouds roll by.

Chapter 1

THE GEOGRAPHY OF KENTUCKY

When people wander around Kentucky, they interact with one of the coolest ongoing science projects ever! Kentucky is chemistry and physics in action.

Ancient Geology

If humans had lived in Kentucky 485 million years ago, they would have needed gills. That's because a shallow sea covered the land. When sea animals died, their shells and bones mixed with sand and mud. Over time, this turned into a soft rock called limestone.

Back then, the continents were one giant landmass called Pangaea. Under the ocean, huge chunks of rock called tectonic plates crashed into each other. This gradually caused the land and climate to change.

About 360 million years ago, the land that is now Kentucky moved close to the equator. The sea shrank, and swamps formed. Plants died and decayed into a soggy mix called peat. After tens of millions of years, Pangaea broke apart. The land that is now Kentucky drifted north. The climate cooled. Rushing rivers brought heavy clay and sand. The weight mashed down layers of peat. Ultimately, the peat hardened and turned into coal.

Spelunkers stand in front of the New Discovery borehole in Mammoth Cave. The cave system is the largest in the world. It's so big that people still haven't explored all of it.

The sea dried up around 325 million years ago. Limestone at its bottom became exposed. Rivers washed over the rocks and seeped into cracks. In time, small openings turned into canyons, and water dripped on limestone still underground. The pressure created tiny tunnels. Those tunnels became larger until they turned into massive rooms. Today, we see the results in Mammoth Cave. It's the largest cave system in the world!

All this time, another amazing thing was happening. Two hundred million years of tectonic activity had pushed land upward. This turned into the Appalachian Mountains. The range stretches from eastern Canada to Alabama. Hikers in the Appalachians walk over one of the oldest mountain ranges on the planet.

Kentucky's Five Regions

Kentucky's five regions are so unique, they are almost like five different states.

Eastern Coal Field

Eastern Kentucky has jagged mountains and mighty forests. This region takes up one-fourth of the state. Seventy-five percent of the state's coal can be found here. Aboveground, the Licking, Cumberland, and Kentucky rivers flow. Millions of years of hydropower pounded the rocks, creating natural bridges, plunging gorges, and immense formations. Climbers hike to Kentucky's highest point, Black Mountain, which is 4,145 feet (1,264 meters) high. It's found south of the Daniel Boone National Forest near the Tennessee border.

Bluegrass

When people think of Kentucky, many picture the Bluegrass Region. Here are the famous green plains, blue skies, and miles of white fences surrounding horse ranches. The Ohio River is the northern border. To the south, steep hills called the Knobs separate the area from other regions.

Bluegrass is green. It probably got its name from its buds, which are a dark shade in spring. Lots of people think bluegrass comes from Kentucky, but it isn't native to the state. Folklore says an early settler brought the seeds in a thimble. Most likely, French traders brought bluegrass with them when they explored the Ohio River Valley in the mid-1600s.

When the sun shines over Kentucky's Cumberland Falls, the mist creates a rainbow on most days. If the moon shines brightly enough, it can create a moonbow, too!

Early settlers built port towns like Louisville along the river. Louisville is Kentucky's largest city. The state capital, Frankfurt, is in the heart of the Bluegrass Region. So is Lexington, the second-largest city and home of the University of Kentucky.

Pennyroyal

The Pennyroyal Region got its name from the tiny purple flowers that bloom everywhere there. The region runs along the Tennessee border and north to the Knobs. It's home to Mammoth Cave. Some rooms of the cave are big enough for concerts. Boats can coast through other parts!

Big Bone Lick

After the ancient sea dried up, it left soft and salty clay in a wetland south of the Ohio River. These places are called salt licks.

Animals need salt to stay healthy. Twelve thousand years ago, mammoths, ground sloths, mastodons, and other animals came to lick the salty clay. Many animals died there, likely killed by people for their meat and skins. Their bones stayed behind, stuck in the heavy clay.

In 1739, French explorer Baron Charles Le Moyne de Longueuil visited the salt lick. He wrote about its massive bones and teeth. Soon, people started calling it Big Bone Lick.

Visitors collected samples for experts to study. Nobody knew what to think. Many believed the huge bones came from elephants, but the tusks grew the wrong way. The molars were the size of elephant teeth, but they were shaped like those of meat-eaters. Elephants didn't live so far north.

There were other confusing bones. They looked similar to known animals, but they were different in important ways. People wondered if the fossils were from animals that nobody had seen before.

Throughout the early 1800s, scientists wondered if the Great Flood described in the Bible killed these animals. In 1859, *The Origin of Species* was published. In it, Charles Darwin talked about the theory of evolution—or how animals and plants might have changed, or evolved, over a long time. It defied many people's beliefs about how the world was created.

Today, scientists call Big Bone Lick a marvel. It's a record of evolution in action. It's also the birthplace of American paleontology. Ongoing research reveals more data about extinct animals and what might have happened to them. People still debate the theory of evolution. Big Bone Lick became part of the Kentucky State Park System in 1960. It's also part of the Lewis and Clark National Historic Trail.

The area has two of the largest lakes east of the Mississippi River. Kentucky Lake and Lake Barkley were made by the damming of the Tennessee and Cumberland rivers. It created an island in the middle of the state. People fish, ski, and camp at the Land Between the Lakes National Recreation Area.

Western Coal Field

In the northwest corner of the state lies the Western Coal Field. It's part of the U.S. Interior Coal Field. Aboveground, farmers raise tobacco, soybeans, wheat, and other crops. Hogs and beef cattle feed on the delicious grasses. The Western Coal Field is south of the Ohio River and east of the Mississippi River.

Jackson's Purchase

In 1818, General Andrew Jackson made a deal with the Chickasaw people. Kentucky gained 2,400 square miles (6,216 square kilometers) of swampy land in the southwestern corner of the state. Jackson's Purchase is cut off from the rest of the state by water. The Ohio and Mississippi rivers border Illinois and Missouri. People can enter it by land only through Tennessee.

Flora and Fauna

Kentucky is a fisherman's paradise. There are 89,431 miles (143,925 km) of rivers and streams. In the water swim dozens of fish like trout, bass, carp, and catfish. All that water and nutrient-rich soil also make a perfect home for more than 3,500 kinds of plants.

Forests filled with oaks, sycamores, maples, and pines cover almost half the state. The tulip poplar is the state tree. Its leaves are shaped like tulip petals. At one time, Kentucky leaders thought that the

The fire pink's bright blooms attract attention, but its sticky leaves trap insects that fly too close. That's why they are also called catchfly.

Kentucky coffee tree should be the state tree. It got its name from settlers who roasted its seeds to create a coffeelike drink.

Goldenrod is Kentucky's state flower. Its fringelike petals make a sunshine bloom. The Kentucky glade cress is a tiny wildflower that only blooms in Bullitt and Jefferson counties. The fire pink flower is also called catchfly. Its sticky leaves trap insects. The Kentucky lady slipper orchid is among the rarest flowers in the world.

All of that water and food attracts animals. Elk, wild turkeys, bobcats, and white-tailed deer roam the state. Bald eagles, hawks, and hundreds of other species soar in the sky. Bats fill the caves. But unchecked hunting killed off some animals. Bison, wolves, and panthers no longer live in Kentucky. Black bears disappeared about one hundred years ago. They are coming back, though, thanks to conservation efforts. Kentucky truly is a wonderland!

Chapter 2

THE HISTORY OF KENTUCKY

Some people think Daniel Boone discovered Kentucky, but that's not correct. French explorers like Jacques Marquette and Louis Jolliet traveled the Ohio River before Boone was even born. Nearly twelve thousand years before that, the first Paleo-Indian societies arrived. They hunted animals and gathered food that grew wild. In time, they learned to farm squash, gourds, sunflowers, and corn.

Around one thousand years ago, Mound Builders called the Mississippians arrived. They built a village near where the Ohio and Mississippi rivers cross. They buried their dead with pottery, treasures, and other items. They left about 350 years later. Nobody knows why. Native tribes later used Kentucky for hunting grounds.

The 1700s: More Elbow Room

In the 1700s, New England was becoming crowded. More settlers arrived each year. Legend says Daniel Boone explored new lands because he needed "more elbow room"!

Settlers pushed west. The Appalachian Mountains made a mighty roadblock. In 1750, Dr. Thomas Walker learned about a trail wide enough to travel by horse. Native people had used it for hundreds of

Daniel Boone was one of Kentucky's greatest explorers. He led settlers along the Wilderness Road through the dangerous Cumberland Pass. He also built Fort Boonesborough.

years. Walker found it in southern Virginia. He named it Cumberland Gap, after Britain's popular Prince William, Duke of Cumberland.

In this new land, long hunters like Boone and James Harrod found 25 million acres (10 million hectares) of forest to explore. In 1774, Harrod, his brother Samuel, and thirty other men built Kentucky's first permanent settlement. They called it Harrodsburg. Boone and his men built Fort Boonesborough the next year. Many people braved the Cumberland Gap. Others rode rafts down the Ohio River. Many brought slaves. Slaves cleared fields for crops and helped defend forts.

Settlers battled with native tribes over food and land. Wounds and diseases killed many. The Revolutionary War killed more. Great Britain promised land to several tribes if they fought the white settlers. At that time, Kentucky County was part of Virginia. Virginia's government couldn't send help. Native warriors kidnapped several people, including Boone. A few, like Boone's son James, were killed.

After the war ended, Kentucky County citizens asked to form their own state. Kentucky became America's fifteenth state on June 1, 1792. By 1796, Boone and others had widened Wilderness Road. Wagonloads of people came to make Kentucky their home.

The 1800s: Prosperity and Pain

By 1803, one in every four Kentuckians was a slave. Some people thought slavery was necessary. Others thought it was wrong. Abolitionists like Kentucky's second governor, James Garrard, worked hard to end slavery. In 1833, Kentucky passed the Non-Importation Act. This law said it was illegal to buy slaves only to resell them.

Ohio and Indiana were free states on the other side of the Ohio River. Louisville and other river cities became the last stop on the Underground Railroad. The railroad wasn't underground or even a railroad. It was people, both whites and free blacks, who helped thousands of runaway slaves escape to freedom.

In 1861, several slave states wanted to form their own country. Kentucky stayed in the Union, but some people supported the Confederate states. Kentucky was important to both sides. It bordered Union and Confederate states. Its rivers carried goods to markets in the South. It's rumored that President Abraham Lincoln once said, "I hope to have God on my side, but I need Kentucky."

Kentucky Derby

Legend says the first Kentucky horse race happened in 1783. Two men raced down Market Street in Louisville. Back then, quarter horses were raised in Kentucky. These horses were fast and strong. In time, the elegant thoroughbreds became the more popular breed.

In the 1800s, jockey clubs and racetracks sprang up throughout Kentucky. Young Colonel M. Lewis Clark, the grandson of explorer William Clark, had a dream. He wanted a glamorous racetrack to show off Kentucky's world-famous racehorses. His dream came true when he opened Churchill Downs in Lexington.

The first Kentucky Derby ran in 1875. Oliver Lewis, an African American jockey, won while riding Aristides. African American jockeys won fifteen of the next twenty-eight races. Ben Ali was the first horse to wear the famed garland of 554 roses in 1896.

African American Jimmy Winkfield is a racing legend. He rode in four races. Winkfield and His Eminence won the roses in 1901. The next year, he won again riding Alan-a-Dale. The race was Winkfield's last at Churchill Downs. A year later, only white jockeys could enter the derby.

In 2000, Marlon St. Julien was the first African American jockey to ride in the Kentucky Derby since Winkfield. The whites-only policy ended, but the derby holds onto other customs.

Each year on the first Saturday in May, horses run for the roses. The University of Louisville Marching Band still plays Stephen Foster's "My Old Kentucky Home." Jockeys parade the horses before the grandstand. People sip mint juleps. They eat burgoo, a thick stew of beef, chicken, pork, and vegetables. Women wear their finest spring clothes and oversized hats. Thousands flood the center field to cheer their favorite thoroughbred. The derby remains a true Kentucky tradition.

Some families were torn apart. Kentucky senator John Crittenden's two sons were generals—one for the North and one for the South. About seventy-five thousand Kentucky men and boys wore Union blue uniforms. Thirty-five thousand or so wore Confederate gray.

Kentucky-born men even led the two governments. Lincoln was born in what is now Hodgenville. William Jefferson Davis, president of the Confederate states, was born in Christian County. Almost eleven thousand Kentucky soldiers died before the Civil War ended in 1865.

Kentucky's river cities were important stops on the Underground Railroad. People like Harriet Tubman helped thousands of slaves escape into northern states and Canada.

Like other slave states, Kentucky suffered after the war. Farms had been destroyed. People had to rebuild businesses and roads. Some thought black people shouldn't get jobs or land that white people could have. The Ku Klux Klan was a secret society of white people. Some Klan members damaged or destroyed black-owned homes and businesses. They harassed black people and those who sympathized with them. Many people were even killed.

A number of people didn't agree with the Klan. In 1866, antislavery activists John G. Fee and Cassius M. Clay started Berea College.

Fort Knox stores more than thirty-six thousand bars of gold! It has guarded other treasures, too. During World War II, the government stored the Constitution and the Declaration of Independence there.

It was America's first integrated college. Blacks and whites could learn and work together.

The 1900s: Changing Times

At the start of the twentieth century, more and more goods came from factories. Factories needed coal. Kentucky's miners dug deeper. Wars in Europe rattled the country. The Great Depression of the 1930s weighed heavy on America. Many people lost their jobs and homes.

But Kentuckians are strong. They fought hard to survive. In 1933, President Franklin D. Roosevelt put his New Deal into action. The Tennessee Valley Authority put lots of people to work. For eleven years, people built dams in Kentucky's rivers. The dams prevented flooding and generated electricity.

Kentucky turned into the richest state in January 1937. That's when Fort Knox became the United States' gold depository. More than thirty-six thousand gold bars are stored there. Each weighs about 27.5 pounds (12.5 kilograms)!

Rights for All

During the first half of the 1900s, segregation meant that whites and blacks lived apart. They had different churches, schools, and businesses. Things were supposed to be "separate but equal," but usually they weren't.

After World War I, more people supported groups like the Ku Klux Klan. In the 1950s and 1960s, black and white people marched to protest segregation. Thousands of black people registered to vote. Some were killed for their beliefs. The Kentucky Commission on Civil Rights started in 1960. Six years later, it was the first state south of the Mason-Dixon Line to pass a civil rights act.

Kentucky's beginning was harsh. Its growth was sometimes painful. Still, a powerful bond keeps Kentuckians proud of their history.

Chapter 3

THE GOVERNMENT OF KENTUCKY

America is strong because its people choose who will run the government. The United States' government has three branches. Each has different powers to keep the government balanced.

Laws keep citizens safe. Congress is our legislative branch. It writes laws. The Senate and the House of Representatives make up Congress. Each state elects people to serve in Congress.

The executive branch is the president. The president puts laws into action through federal agencies. The vice president becomes president if ever needed.

The judicial branch enforces laws based on the Constitution. Nine Supreme Court judges make up this branch. They give opinions about what laws mean.

State governments have legislative, executive, and judicial branches, too. Officially, Kentucky isn't a state. Like Virginia, Massachusetts, and Pennsylvania, Kentucky calls itself a commonwealth. Commonwealth governments function the same way as state governments, but in a commonwealth, emphasis is placed on government based on the will and consent of the people.

Kentucky has had four state constitutions since it entered the Union in 1792. The most recent version was written in 1891.

The Old Governor's Mansion in Frankfort is one of the oldest official residences in the country. It's two years older than the White House. Today, the lieutenant governor lives there.

Kentucky's Executive Branch

The governor heads the executive branch. Governors oversee several departments and cabinets. For example, Kentucky has departments for economic development, public safety, agriculture, education, and transportation. The lieutenant governor, secretary of state, treasurer, and auditor all work with the governor.

Governors and other executive officials serve four-year terms. They must be at least thirty years old and have lived in Kentucky for six years.

Education in Kentucky

Once upon a time, children didn't always go to school. It sounds like a fairy tale. But just over a hundred years ago, it was a way of life in Kentucky. Farming families needed children to work in the fields and do chores. Still, Kentucky's leaders wanted good schools.

The first public schools opened in 1838. Tax money helped pay for teachers, books, buildings, and more. Many children in rural and mountain areas attended only once in a while, if at all. Students didn't always graduate. As the country became more industrialized, more people moved into cities. In the early 1920s, education for children became required by law. For a long time, blacks and whites attended separate schools. This was called segregation. The U.S. Supreme Court ruled in 1954 that segregation in public schools was illegal. Still whites and blacks lived in different areas and usually attended different schools. Some schools were quite poor. In the 1970s, Louisville worked hard to make sure its schools became desegregated.

Kentucky students had fallen behind. They scored below the national average on standardized tests. Too many dropped out. Some schools were quite poor. Kentucky's students needed help.

In 1988, Kentucky courts ruled that state money had not been divided fairly among schools. Wealthier neighborhoods received more money. At that time, one in three adults in Kentucky hadn't graduated from high school. The Kentucky Education Reform Act of 1990 gave local schools more control and increased funding.

By 2004, Kentucky's teacher-to-student ratio was the fifteenth best in the nation. Test scores in math and reading have improved. Graduation rates are rising. Kentucky's schools are growing stronger.

Kentucky's Legislative Branch

The legislative branch has two parts: the senate and the house of representatives. They are called the general assembly. They make and pass Kentucky laws.

The Kentucky General Assembly is made up of thirty-eight state senators and one hundred state representatives. They make and pass laws to help Kentucky's citizens stay safe and prosper.

To make a state law, legislators first write a bill. Senators and representatives discuss the bill. They make changes if necessary before they vote on it. A majority of representatives and senators must approve the bill. Then they send it to the governor. If the governor approves, the bill becomes a law. If the governor doesn't approve, it is considered vetoed. The bill goes back to the general assembly. The process starts over.

Kentucky has thirty-eight state senators and one hundred state representatives. State representatives must be at least twenty-four years old. They must have lived in Kentucky for two years and in their districts for one year. State representatives serve for two years. State senators must be at least thirty years old. They must have lived in Kentucky for six years and in their districts for one year. State senators serve for four years.

Kentucky's Judicial Branch

Kentucky's many city and county courts make up its judicial branch. Criminal courts deal with people who break laws. Civil courts handle disputes that don't involve crimes. Instead, they focus on lawsuits. Both courts use state and national laws to resolve problems.

Some important positions in the judicial branch are the attorney general and judges. The attorney general's office prosecutes crime. Judges serve in district, circuit, or appeals courts. Kentucky, like all states, has its own supreme court. County attorneys, justices of the peace, sheriffs, and jailers are elected, too.

In America, people are considered innocent until proven guilty. Lots of people believe a jury is the best way to decide guilt or innocence. A jury is a group of citizens who live or work in the same area. They listen to the facts of a case. Judges sentence people if juries find them guilty. In civil cases, juries decide who is right. They decide if one person should pay damages to another. Some people don't want a jury trial. In these cases, judges make the final decisions.

District attorneys and judges must be at least thirty years old and have practiced law for eight years. They must have lived in Kentucky for two years. Judges also must have lived in their district for two years. Attorney generals and district court judges serve four-year terms. All other judges serve eight years.

Local Government

Local governments run smaller areas where people work and live. There are county and city or township governments.

Kentucky has 120 counties. County governments keep records on who gets married or divorced, who owns property such as cars or homes, and all babies born in that county. They operate sheriffs' departments and county jails. County commissioners lead county governments.

City or township governments make decisions for their city or town. For example, they plan budgets for police and fire departments. They decide where people can build homes or set up businesses. They repair roads, curbs, and sidewalks. They have departments for parks and recreation and public safety. Mayors lead city governments.

County and city governments are usually separate. Sometimes they join together for what's called a metropolitan government. Metropolitan governments make sure that cities and counties don't duplicate jobs. This can make local government more efficient. In 2003, Louisville and Jefferson County joined. As a result, Louisville became the sixteenth-largest city in the United States.

Federal Government

Two senators from each state serve in the Senate. The number of representatives depends on the state's population. Kentucky has six U.S. representatives. U.S. senators serve for six years. Representatives run for reelection every two years.

Kentucky has eight electoral votes for presidential elections—one for each of its representatives and senators. Eight Kentuckians called electorates are chosen for the electoral college. Electorates usually vote for whoever received the most votes in their state. The president is officially elected by the electoral college, not the general election in November.

Chapter 4

THE ECONOMY OF
KENTUCKY

People around the world use Kentucky goods. They burn its coal. Some smoke tobacco. Others race horses. Many more drive its machines. Until 1970, most Kentuckians were farmers. Nowadays, manufacturing creates the most jobs and revenue. In 2007, Kentucky shipped goods worth more than $19 billion to Canada, France, Mexico, Japan, and other countries. Ninety-seven percent of them were manufactured goods.

Living Off the Land

Settlers in the late 1700s found Kentucky's soil perfect for hemp and tobacco. People used hemp to make paper, rope, and cloth. Tobacco was always in demand. Farmers grew food for their families and livestock. They shipped goods on the country's first superhighways—the Ohio and Mississippi rivers. By 1860, Kentucky grew more tobacco than any other state.

In the early 1900s, tobacco companies tried to pay farmers a lower price. Some farmers refused to sell unless companies paid more. Others couldn't lose that income. In 1904, fighting broke out in the Black Patch district of western Kentucky. Some farmers who didn't want to sell snuck into the fields of those who did. These night rangers burned barns and crops. The Black Patch War lasted almost five years. The governor sent in army troops to stop it. In the end, tobacco companies agreed to pay better prices.

Corn also thrived in the rich soil. Resourceful farmers cooked the extra to create Kentucky bourbon whiskey. In time, there were hundreds of distilleries around the state.

Jockey Calvin Borel and Mine That Bird wear a blanket of roses in the winner's circle at Churchill Downs. The pair won the 2009 Kentucky Derby.

Livestock love the fertile land, too. Cattle, sheep, and pigs feed upon lush grasses, but in Kentucky the horse is king. The first thoroughbred arrived in 1779. Soon, horse breeding became a booming business. The Bluegrass Region's sprawling meadows made perfect ranches. Its trainers were skilled and had horse smarts. Racing clubs sprang up everywhere.

Today, many of the world's finest horses come from Kentucky. Luxury stables house thousands of thoroughbreds. The Kentucky Derby draws more than 150,000 people each May.

Logging and Coal

In the 1800s, loggers harvested Kentucky's mighty trees. By 1905, people worried that the forests would be lost forever. Some spots were cut down so completely that nothing was left to grow. Logging

Coal Mining in Kentucky

Coal mining is filthy, suffocating, damp, and backbreaking work. In the industry's earliest days, miners dug in darkness, sometimes crouched in tight spaces and sometimes covered in muddy water. Cave-ins, explosions, and poisonous fumes killed many. Black lung disease, caused by breathing in coal dust, killed even more.

The state's first commercial coal mine, McLean Drift Bank, opened in 1820. The first Mine Ventilation Law passed in 1880. By 1890, the United Mine Workers Union was working to improve conditions. Despite their efforts, there were 305 coal mine disasters between 1901 and 1925. The worst happened in 1907. An explosion killed 362 miners in West Virginia.

In 1970, thirty-eight miners in Hyden, Kentucky, died in a mine explosion. Two years later, 180 miners in Harlan County went on strike. They demanded safer working conditions, better wages, and fair labor practices. The strike turned violent in 1973, when a young miner named Lawrence Jones was killed in a scuffle with two coal company guards.

Three years later in Oven Fork, twenty-six miners died in an explosion. Fourteen widows successfully sued the Scotia Coal Company for retribution. The Federal Mine Safety and Health Act of 1977 made great strides toward improved mine safety.

Modern mines have better ventilation and escape procedures. The Mine Improvement and New Emergency Response (MINER) Act of 2006 put more rescue policies in place. Escapeways must be within thirty minutes' walking time. Self-rescuers must provide two hours of air for each miner. Refuge and barricade chambers stock water, self-rescuers, and seals.

Scientists are working on effective tracking methods and better communication equipment. Technology can help trapped miners stay alive until they can be rescued. Disasters and deaths have dropped in the last decades, but the job remains dangerous. In 2006, an explosion killed five Kentucky miners in Holmes Mill. Each year, about a thousand miners die of black lung disease.

dried up by the first half of the twentieth century. It took decades to rebuild. Today, Kentucky's Division of Forestry works hard to preserve forests. It improved fire prevention and response programs. Its nurseries grow saplings to replace harvested trees. The logging business boomed again by the late twentieth century.

Many people say surface mining, like this site on Black Mountain, destroys the environment. Reclamation laws mean mining companies must leave healthy land behind when they're done.

Mining had been steady work since before the Civil War. Things changed once World War I started. Factories that made weapons and machinery needed lots of coal. Farmers put down their plows and grabbed pickaxes. The coal business dropped off after the war ended in 1918, but it picked up again during World War II.

Mining was dirty and dangerous. It also damaged the land. Strip or surface mining, first done in 1866, became common in the mid-twentieth century. Miners used giant machines to remove soil and rock. Sometimes entire mountaintops were dug away.

People said mining destroyed mountain environments and polluted rivers. How could the government protect the land and miners without the loss of jobs or business income? In 1977, the United States passed the Surface Mining Control and Reclamation Act. Mining companies had to reclaim the land, or make sure that it was usable and healthy when they were done with it.

Moving Forward

An elk roams a wildlife preserve in Kentucky. Males lose their antlers in March and begin to grow them back in May for the mating season in late summer.

Manufacturing in Lexington, Louisville, and other big cities boomed in the twentieth century. From 1930 to 1970, lots of folks left their farms for the cities. Factories churned out farm and transportation machinery, chemicals, metals, computers, and other electronic products. Toyota opened a plant in Georgetown in 2006 and created thousands of jobs. Transportation equipment was Kentucky's top export in 2007.

Working for the People

Kentucky is home to two important military bases. Fort Knox does more than store gold. It's also home to the U.S. Army's Armored Warfare Training Center. Fort Campbell is home to the Screaming Eagles—the 101st Airborne Division.

Service industries are also important. Instead of growing or building things, service workers help people. Firemen and police, teachers and nurses, shop workers, and even the people who take orders at the drive-through window are part of the service industry.

People from other states and countries visit the Mammoth Cave, Land Between the Lakes, and Cumberland Gap National Park.

Chapter 5

PEOPLE FROM KENTUCKY: PAST AND PRESENT

Trailblazers like Dr. Thomas Walker, Daniel Boone, James Harrod, and George Rogers Clark built Kentucky. Many kinds of trailblazers have called Kentucky home.

Kentucky Trailblazers

Garrett A. Morgan (1877–1963) Paris, Kentucky, native Garrett A. Morgan was the son of former slaves. He built a gas mask in 1916. Three years later, he used it to rescue men trapped in an underground tunnel beneath Lake Erie. Then World War I soldiers used his mask design. Morgan also patented the first automatic three-position traffic signal in 1923.

Colonel Sanders (1890–1980) The tastiest trailblazer of all was Colonel Harland Sanders. His secret recipe of eleven herbs and spices fried in a pressure cooker created juicy chicken. Started in Corbin, Kentucky, Kentucky Fried Chicken was one of the first franchised eateries in the world. Colonel Sanders died in 1980, but the words "finger-lickin' good" live on. Though he was called a colonel, Sanders never served in the military. The governor of Kentucky gave him the honorary title in 1935.

Franklin R. Sousley (1925– 1945) Private First Class Franklin R. Sousley of Flemingsburg, Kentucky, helped raise the U.S. flag at Iwo Jima during World War II. Nineteen-year-old Sousley was killed in action less than a month later. People remember his and all soldiers' heroism every time they see the famous photograph of the flag raising. They can also see him at the U.S. Marine Corps War Memorial in Washington, D.C.

Colonel Harlan Sanders will forever be the face of Kentucky. His famous white hair, suit, and beard are known around the world. He had several jobs, but cooking was his favorite.

Politicians

Louis Brandeis (1856–1941) Justice Louis Brandeis was the first Jewish judge to serve on the Supreme Court. He was born in Louisville, Kentucky. Brandeis University in Waltham, Massachusetts, was named after him.

Henry Clay (1777–1852) Kentucky senator Henry Clay was called the Great Compromiser. In 1820, Maine and Missouri wanted to enter the Union. To keep Congress balanced, he proposed the Missouri Compromise. Missouri entered as a slave state and Maine as a free state. Clay later helped draft the Compromise of 1850. It let California enter the Union as a free state, but it included the Fugitive Slave Act. Clay's compromises helped delay the Civil War.

President Zachary Taylor's gruff, no-nonsense approach as an army general earned him the nickname Old Rough and Ready.

John Marshall Harlan (1833–1911) U.S. Supreme Court Justice John Marshall Harlan was born in Boyle County. Harlan was the lone judge who disagreed when the court ruled that "separate but equal" was fair. Harlan wrote in his dissent that "Our Constitution is color blind, and neither knows nor tolerates classes among citizens."

Zachary Taylor (1784–1850) Abraham Lincoln wasn't the only Kentucky son to serve as president. Zachary Taylor grew up near Louisville. Taylor fought against the British in the War of 1812. He also fought in the Mexican-American War in the 1840s. Fellow soldiers nicknamed him Old Rough and Ready. He was elected president in 1848. Taylor died sixteen months after he took office.

Other Inspirational Kentuckians

John James Audubon (1785–1851) Birds flitting about western Kentucky inspired artist John James Audubon. He

Pioneers on the Underground Railroad

Thornton and Lucie Blackburn were slaves in Louisville in the early 1800s. They belonged to different owners. Lucie's owner died shortly after she and Thornton married. A local merchant bought her and made plans to sell her. Resold slaves often went to owners in the Deep South.

On July 11, 1831, the Blackburns escaped before Lucie could be resold. They used forged papers that said they were free. They rode a ferry across the Ohio River into Indiana, a free state.

They ended up in Detroit, Michigan, where many free blacks lived. Lucie's new owner found them two years later. Thornton and Lucie were arrested. Detroit's antislavery society helped them: Lettia French visited Lucie in jail, and they switched clothes. French stayed in the jail cell while a disguised Lucie walked out the door, escaping to Canada that night.

The next day, police tried to take Thornton to his owners. A group of armed citizens, both black and white, attacked the sheriff. Amid the confusion, Thornton escaped. The events were called the Blackburn Riots.

Thornton and Lucie found each other in Canada. Their owners tried to have them extradited, or returned, to Kentucky, but Canadian officials refused. Its governors said slavery was a terrible fate. That decision helped future runaway slaves stay in Canada.

The Blackburns lived in Toronto and built a successful cab business. Thornton snuck back into Kentucky to help his mother and brother escape.

In 1985, Underground Railroad historians dug up a corner of Sackville Street School in Toronto. The Blackburns' home had stood there more than a hundred years before. They found artifacts that likely belonged to Thornton and Lucie. In 1999, the Canadian government designated the Blackburns Persons of National Historic Significance. Officials in Toronto and Louisville erected plaques in their honor in 2002.

started drawing and writing *Birds in America* when he lived near Henderson.

William Wells Brown (1814–1884) Words inspired other Kentuckians. William Wells Brown was America's first black novelist. He escaped from slavery in 1834, and he published his memoir in 1847.

Duncan Hines (1880–1959) Food inspired Duncan Hines. He was a real person, not just a cake mix! The Bowling Green, Kentucky, native wrote reviews about his favorite restaurants and hotels that he found as a traveling salesman. In the mid-1930s, "Recommended by Duncan Hines" was a gold star.

The First Lady of Country Music, Loretta Lynn, grew up in poverty. Her father worked in the coal mines of Butcher Hollow.

Loretta Lynn (1935–) Years after country music became popular, a coal miner's daughter would bring her own style to it. Lynn was born in Butcher Hollow, the second of eight children. She scored a major hit with "Coal Miner's Daughter." A biographical movie by the same name was released in 1980.

Bill Monroe (1911–1996) Appalachian music inspired Bill Monroe. He learned to play the mandolin when he was a young boy in Rosine. His band the Bluegrass Boys, named for Kentucky's famous bluegrass, played a speedy rendition of the folk tune "Mule Skinner Blues" at the Grand Ole Opry in 1939. A new music style was born. Bluegrass combines blues, gospel, and folk music with traditional mountain instruments like the banjo, violin, and mandolin.

Helen Thomas (1920–) Helen Thomas has been a White House correspondent since 1961. The Winchester-born Thomas has written about ten presidents. She gets the best seat—the front row—in the Press Room and always asks the first question.

Kentuckians with Competitive Spirit

Muhammad Ali (1942–) Perhaps the greatest champ to come from Louisville is Muhammad Ali. Born Cassius Clay in 1942, Ali converted to Islam in the 1960s. He changed his name shortly after he won the gold medal in boxing at the 1960 Olympics. He liked to say that he could "float like a butterfly, sting like a bee." Ali earned the heavyweight championship title three times. He retired in 1981. Three years later, he was diagnosed with Parkinson's disease. Ali received the Presidential Medal of Freedom in 2005.

"Pee Wee" Reese (1918–1999) Harold Henry Reese was a Louisville marbles champion long before he played shortstop and third base for the Brooklyn (later Los Angeles) Dodgers.

Reese led the team to a World Series title in 1955.

Wes Unseld (1946–)

Louisville, Kentucky, produced another admired ball handler. Wesley Unseld led the University of Louisville basketball team to two NCAA tournaments. He's considered one of the fifty greatest NBA players of all time.

Michael Waltrip (1963–)

Kentuckians have strong spirits, which makes for tough competitors. Owensboro native Michael Waltrip is a two-time Daytona 500 winner. Older brother Darrell won the Winston Cup title three times in his career.

Boxing legend Muhammad Ali is from Louisville. Ali is an Olympic gold medalist and three-time heavyweight champ. He received the Presidential Medal of Freedom in 2005.

Timeline

1673	French explorer Jacques Marquette explores the Mississippi River.
1739	Captain Le Moyne de Longueuil finds massive fossils at Big Bone Lick.
1750	Thomas Walker learns about a trail through the Appalachian Mountains used by Native Americans. He names it the Cumberland Gap.
1769	Daniel Boone and John Finley explore the land west of the Appalachians.
1774	James Harrod builds Fort Harrod, the first permanent settlement.
1775	Daniel Boone widens the Wilderness Trail and establishes Fort Boonesborough.
1792	Kentucky becomes the fifteenth state on June 1, 1792. It enters the Union as a proslavery state.
1830	The Louisville and Portland Canal opens.
1833	Kentucky passes a law that bans people from importing slaves for resale to southern states.
1862	Union and Confederate soldiers fight the Battle of Perryville. Kentucky remains under Union control for the rest of the war.
1875	The first Kentucky Derby runs at Churchill Downs.
1891	Kentucky adopts its present state constitution.
1900	More than 1,500 armed civilians take control of the state capitol for two weeks; an assassin kills Governor William Goebel.
1933	The Tennessee Valley Authority begins building dams in Kentucky.
1936	Fort Knox becomes the U.S. gold depository.
1966	Kentucky is the first southern state to pass a comprehensive civil rights law.
1977	The Surface Mining Control and Reclamation Act passes.
1990	Kentucky passes the Kentucky Education Reform Act.
2006	Toyota begins building hybrid Camrys in Georgetown, Kentucky.
2009	The National Forest Service closes caves and mines in the southwestern states, including Kentucky, to protect bats from a fungal disease.

State motto:	"United We Stand, Divided We Fall"
State capital:	Frankfort
State tree:	Tulip poplar
State bird:	Cardinal
State flower:	Goldenrod
State fruit or vegetable:	Blackberry
Statehood date and number:	June 1, 1792; fifteenth state
State nickname:	The Bluegrass State
Total area and U.S. rank:	40,411 square miles (104,664 sq km); thirty-seventh-largest state
Population:	4,269,000
Highest elevation:	Black Mountain, at 4,139 feet (1,261 m)
Lowest elevation:	Mississippi River, at 257 feet (78 m)

State flag

State seal

Major rivers:	Ohio River, Mississippi River, Kentucky River, Green River, Cumberland River
Major lakes:	Kentucky Lake, Lake Barkley, Lake Cumberland
Highest recorded temperature:	114 degrees Farenheit (46 degrees Celsius) at Greensburg, on July 28, 1930
Lowest recorded temperature:	-37°F (3°C) at Shelbyville, on January 19, 1994
Origin of state name:	From the Iroquoian word *kenhta-ke*, which means "meadow"
Chief agricultural products:	Tobacco, soybeans, corn, horses, cattle, hogs, dairy
Major industries:	Transportation equipment, coal, tobacco, chemical products, electric equipment, food processing, machinery

Cardinal

Goldenrod

abolitionist A person who is against slavery.

artifact An object made and used by people from long ago.

black lung disease A potentially fatal disease caused by breathing in coal dust.

commonwealth A state that is governed by the people who live there.

dissent A difference of opinion; to disagree.

distill To trickle down; to purify or concentrate; to extract an essence.

escapeway A passage designed for escape.

excavate To dig up or hollow out; to unearth.

extradite To turn over a fugitive to another country.

fugitive A person who flees.

hydropower Electrical power generated by water force.

integrate To bring together all parts of a whole; to end segregation.

limestone A rock made mostly of calcium, usually from the remains of sea animals.

long hunters A nickname for America's early adventurers who carried rifles and spent many months or even years exploring new land.

paleontology The study of prehistoric life through fossils.

Pangaea Believed to be a supercontinent of all land on Earth before it broke apart around fifty-five million years ago.

Parkinson's disease A brain disorder that impairs muscle coordination and function.

peat Partly decayed plant matter that holds lots of water, usually found in bogs and swamps.

reform To improve; to remove defects.

segregation A policy to separate or set apart, usually by race.

self-rescuer A device used by miners to let them breathe clean air in case of cave-ins or dangerous gas.

strip/surface mining To gather coal by removing huge amounts of dirt and rocks from above.

tectonic plate A huge, solid piece of Earth's crust found below the continents and ocean floors.

Center of Excellence for the Study of African Americans

Kentucky State University Visitor and Information Center

Julian M. Carroll Academic Services Building

400 East Main Street

Frankfort, KY 40601

(502) 597-6000

Web site: http://www.kysu.edu/about/heritage/ceskaa

The Center of Excellence for the Study of African Americans is devoted to collecting, preserving, and sharing materials about African Americans who live in Kentucky or are connected to Kentucky.

Churchill Downs

700 Central Avenue

Louisville, KY 40208

(502) 636-4400

Web site: http://www.churchilldowns.com/about/history

Watch an early-morning workout trackside. Find out about the history of the sport and facility by visiting the Web site.

Kentucky Historical Society

100 W. Broadway

Frankfort, KY 40601

(502) 564-1792

Web site: http://history.ky.gov/index.php

The Kentucky Historical Society celebrates Kentucky's diverse history and people. It collects materials and memories about Kentucky's rich heritage and offers a database for study.

Mammoth Cave National Park

1 Mammoth Cave Parkway

Mammoth Cave, KY 42259

(270) 758-2180

Web site: http://www.nps.gov/maca

Mammoth Cave National Park preserves the cave system and part of the Green River Valley in south central Kentucky. This is the world's longest known cave system.

Ontario Black History Society

10 Adelaide Street East, Suite 402

Toronto, ON M5C 1J3

Canada

(416) 867-9420

Web site: http://blackhistorysociety.ca

The Ontario Black History Society promotes the contributions of black people and their heritage. The nonprofit organization sponsors and supports school studies, conferences and exhibits, and public interest in black history.

Parks Canada National Office

25-7-N Eddy Street

Gatineau, QC K1A 0M5

Canada

(888) 773-8888

Web site: http://www.pc.gc.ca

Parks Canada recognizes several sites that were found to be part of Canada's Underground Railroad. One is the home of former Kentucky slaves Thornton and Lucie Blackburn.

Wickliffe Mounds State Historic Site

94 Green Street

Wickliffe, KY 42087

(270) 335-3681

Web site: http://parks.ky.gov/findparks/histparks/wm

Wickliffe Mounds State Historic Site's museum features pottery and tools made of stone, bone, and shells that were found during excavation. Visitors can learn about the Mississippian architecture and burial practices and get a stunning view of the village from the ceremonial mound.

Web Sites

Due to the nature of Internet links, Rosen Publishing has developed an online list of Web sites related to the subject of this book. This site is updated regularly. Please use this link to access the list:

http://www.rosenlinks.com/uspp/kypp

Burton, K. Melissa, and James Asher. *Kentucky's Boone and the Pioneer Spirit*. Kuttawa, KY: McClanahan Publishing House, 2008.

Casper, Julie Kerr. *Forests: More Than Just Trees* (Natural Resources). New York, NY: Chelsea House, 2007.

Collier, James Lincoln. *The Lincoln You Never Knew*. New York, NY: Children's Press, 2004.

George-Warren, Holly, and Laura Levine. *Honky-Tonk Heroes and Hillbilly Angels: The Pioneers of Country and Western Music*. New York, NY: Houghton Mifflin Books for Children, 2006.

Harness, Cheryl. *The Trailblazing Life of Daniel Boone and How Early Americans Took to the Road*. Washington, DC: National Geographic Children's Books, 2007.

Harrison, David L. *Cave Detectives: Unraveling the Mystery of an Ice Age Cave*. San Francisco, CA: Chronicle Books, 2007.

Haugen, David M. *Coal* (Fueling the Future). Farmington Hills, MI: Greenhaven Press. 2006.

Hubbard, Crystal, and Robert McGuire. *The Last Black King of the Kentucky Derby: The Story of Jimmy Winkfield*. New York, NY: Lee & Lowe Books, 2008.

Marsh, Carole. *The Mystery at the Kentucky Derby*. Peachtree City, GA: Gallopade International, 2004.

Maynard, Charles W. *The Appalachians* (Great Mountain Ranges of the World). New York, NY: PowerKids Press, 2004.

Mitchell, Elizabeth. *Journey to the Bottomless Pit: The Story of Stephen Bishop and Mammoth Cave*. New York, NY: Viking, 2004.

Ransom, Candace. *Horses in the Wind: A Tale of Seabiscuit*. Renton, WA: Mirrorstone, 2007.

Roop, Peter, and Connie Roop. *River Roads West: America's First Highways*. Honesdale, PA: Calkins Creek Books, 2007.

Smith, Charles R., Jr. *Twelve Rounds to Glory: The Story of Muhammad Ali*. Cambridge, MA: Candlewick, 2007.

Stokes, John A., Herman Viola, and Lois Wolfe. *Students on Strike: Jim Crow, Civil Rights, Brown and Me*. Washington, DC: National Geographic Children's Books, 2007.

Thomas, Keltie. *How Basketball Works*. Toronto, Canada: Maple Tree Press, 2005.

Williams, Suzanne M. *Kentucky* (From Sea to Shining Sea). New York, NY: Children's Press, 2008.

Zronik, John Paul. *Daniel Boone: Woodsman of Kentucky*. New York, NY: Crabtree Publishing, 2006.

BIBLIOGRAPHY

Brodowsky, Pamela K., and Tom Philbin. *Two Minutes to Glory: The Official History of the Kentucky Derby*. New York, NY: Collins, 2008.

Brown, Meredith Mason. *Frontiersman: Daniel Boone and the Making of America*. Baton Rouge, LA: Louisiana State University Press, 2008.

Climate Center at Western Kentucky University. "Fact Sheet: Ohio River Floods." Retrieved October 11, 2009 (http://kyclim.wku.edu/factSheets/ohioRiver.htm).

Deady, Kathleen W. *Kentucky Facts and Symbols*. Mankato, MN: Hilltop Books/Capstone Press, 2001.

Frost, Karolyn Smardz. *I've Got a Home in Glory Land: A Lost Tale of the Underground Railroad*. New York, NY: Farrar, Straus and Giroux, 2007.

Hedeen, Stanley. *Big Bone Lick: The Cradle of American Paleontology*. Lexington, KY: University Press of Kentucky, 2008.

Hoffman, Lee H. "Kentucky County History." FreePages.com, 1996. Retrieved May 24, 2009 (http://freepages.genealogy.rootsweb.ancestry.com/~harrisonrep/Census/kycounty.htm).

International Trade Association. "Kentucky: Exports, Jobs and Foreign Investment." August 2009. Retrieved October 23, 2009 (http://www.trade.gov/td/industry/otea/state_reports/kentucky.html).

Johnson, Leland R., and Charles E. Parrish. *Triumph at the Falls: The Louisville and Portland Canal*. Louisville, KY: U.S. Army Corps of Engineers, 2007.

Kentucky Department of Fish and Wildlife Resources. "Kentucky Wildlife Action Plan: Appendix 1.7 Description of Physiographic Regions of Kentucky." September 21, 2005. Retrieved August 30, 2009 (http://fw.ky.gov/kfwis/stwg/Appendix/1.7%20Physiography%20of%20Kentucky.pdf).

Kentucky Department for Library and Archives. "Kentucky State Symbols." January 29, 2008. Retrieved May 22, 2009 (http://www.kdla.ky.gov/resources/KYSymbols.htm).

Kentucky Derby. "African Americans in the Derby." Retrieved May 27, 2009 (http://www.kentuckyderby.com/2002/derby_history/african_americans_in_the_derby/jockeys.html).

Kentucky Elections. "Candidate Qualification Information." October 1, 2008. Retrieved October 13, 2009 (http://www.sos.ky.gov/elections/qualifications).

Kentucky State Data Center. "2008 City Population Estimates." July 1, 2009. Retrieved November 2, 2009 (http://ksdc.louisville.edu).

McDonough, James Lee. *War in Kentucky: From Shiloh to Perryville*. Knoxville, TN: University of Tennessee Press, 1994.

Mendez, Guy. "Kentucky's Underground Railroad: Passage to Freedom." Kentucky Educational Television, 2000. Documentary video and timeline (http://www.ket. org/underground/resources/segments01.htm; http://www.ket.org/underground/ timeline).

NetState: Learn About the 50 States. "Kentucky Almanac." September 18, 2008. Retrieved May 8, 2009 (http://www.netstate.com/states/alma/ky_alma.htm).

Official Site of the Kentucky Department of Travel. "Kentucky Facts: Famous Kentuckians." Retrieved May 13, 2009 (www.kentuckytourism.com/NR/ rdonlyres/87C8162D-3180-4BB4-8318-A844C237E0B6/0/FamousKentuckians.pdf).

Slatalla, Michelle. *The Town on Beaver Creek: The Story of a Lost Kentucky Community*. New York, NY: Random House, 2006.

SportsIllustrated.com "A Feeling of a Lifetime." May 4, 2000. Retrieved July 27, 2009 (http://sportsillustrated.cnn.com/more/horseracing/2000/triplecrown/kentucky/ news/2000/05/04/stjulien_derby_ap).

Stern, Gerald M. *The Scotia Widows: Inside Their Lawsuit Against Big Daddy Coal*. New York, NY: Random House, 2008.

Think Kentucky. "Kentucky Exports (2007) and Foreign Direct Investments (2006)" (http://www.thinkkentucky.com/kyedc/pdfs/kyexport.pdf).

U.S. Census Bureau. "State and County Quick Facts: Kentucky." May 9, 2009. Retrieved May 21, 2009 (http://quickfacts.census.gov/qfd/states/21000.html).

Wheeler, Lonnie. *Blue Yonder: Kentucky, the United State of Basketball*. Wilmington, OH: Orange Frazer Press, 1998.

About the Author

Colleen Ryckert Cook researches and writes about all kinds of interesting things, from abolition to zygospores and then some. She earned degrees in communication studies and journalism from the University of Kansas. When she isn't cheering for her beloved Jayhawks during basketball season, she watches her other favorite team, the Kentucky Wildcats, and writes nonfiction books for teens and children.

Photo Credits

Cover (top left), p. 33 Library of Congress Prints and Photographs Division; cover (top right) © www.istockphoto.com/Melinda Fawver; cover (bottom) Heinz Kluetmeier/Sports Illustrated/Getty Images; pp. 3, 6, 13, 20, 26, 31, 38 © www.istockphoto.com/Brian Swartz; p. 4 (top) © GeoAtlas; p. 7 Stephen Alvarez/National Geographic/Getty Images; p. 9 © www.istockphoto.com/Alexey Stiop; p. 12 Raymond T. Scott; p. 14 MPI/Hulton Archive/Getty Images; p. 17 Jerry Pinkney/National Geographic/Getty Images; pp. 18, 29 © AP Images; p. 21 Newscom; p. 23 Scott J. Ferrell/Congressional Quarterly/Getty Images; p. 27 Bill Frakes/Sports Illustrated/Getty Images; p. 30 Shutterstock.com; p. 32 John Olson/Time & Life Pictures/Getty Images; p. 35 Donald Kravitz/Getty Images; p. 37 Getty Images; p. 39 (left) Courtesy of Robesus, Inc.; p. 40 (left) Adam Jones/The Image Bank/Getty Images; p. 40 (right) © www.istockphoto.com/Nancy Nehring.

Designer: Les Kanturek; Editor: Bethany Bryan;
Photo Researcher: Peter Tomlinson